THE BIG BOOK OF FUN!

NATIONAL GEOGRAPHIC

Since 1888, the National Geographic Society has funded more than 12,000 research, exploration, and preservation projects around the world. The Society receives funds from National Geographic Partners, LLC, funded in part by your purchase. A portion of the proceeds from this book supports this vital work. To learn more, visit natgeo.com/info.

NATIONAL GEOGRAPHIC and Yellow Border Design are trademarks of the National Geographic Society, used under license.

For more information, please visit nationalgeographic.com, call 1-800-647-5463, or write to the following address:

National Geographic Partners
1145 17th Street N.W.
Washington, D.C. 20036-4688 U.S.A.

Visit us online at nationalgeographic.com/books

For librarians and teachers: ngchildrensbooks.org

More for kids from National Geographic: natgeokids.com

For information about special discounts for bulk purchases, please contact National Geographic Books Special Sales: specialsales@natgeo.com

For rights or permissions inquiries, please contact National Geographic Books Subsidiary Rights: bookrights@natgeo.com

ISBN: 978-1-4263-0661-7

Printed in China
18/RRDS/4

Games, Jokes, and More!

p. 12

Pick up your pencil and get ready for 80 pages of interactive, brain-teasing fun. You never know what's going to jump out at you when you flip through these eye-popping games and activities. You might spy a jaguar lurking in the grass, take a wild ride through a water-park maze, laugh at a polar bear slipping on the ice, or spot a troll in a mad scientist's laboratory.

You'll find colorful hidden pictures, "What's wrong with this picture?" games, silly animal photographs, matching games, laugh-out-loud comics, and Funny Fill-ins, in which you make up your own hilarious stories. Test your money savvy when you try to guess the price of a fancy purebred cat or the cost of building the Eiffel Tower. Or take a trivia quiz that could prove you actually *do* know more than your parents. And that's just the beginning of the fun inside *The Big Book of Fun!*

Pulled straight from the pages of NATIONAL GEOGRAPHIC KIDS magazine, these games have been tested and loved by kids everywhere. And as you would expect coming from National Geographic, this book will take you on one adventure after another—traveling into outer space, through the jungle, deep under the sea, and everywhere in between.

p. 42

The best part is that you get to show how smart you are on every page. The answers are at the back of the book, but try to figure out the games on your own before you sneak a peek. And don't forget to share the fun with your family and friends!

p. 46

Table of Contents

p. 26

p. 6

p. 64

OUT of This WORLD

Help Zorb the alien run the errands on the list below and return home. You must obey the rules of his galaxy:

- Fly by each stop on the list and pass the front door if there is one.
- You can't cross your own path or travel the same route twice.
- You do not have to do the errands in the order they are listed, but certain tasks logically come before others.

ERRANDS

✓ Walk Zorb's dog, Comet, at the extra-terrestrial dog park.
✓ Buy green goo at the Green Goo Factory.
✓ Pick up Zorb's little sister at school.
✓ Work out at the Anti-gravity Gym.
✓ Buy pet supplies at the Meteorite Mall.
✓ View the stars at the planetarium.
✓ Drop Zorb's little sister off at the Black Hole Bowling Alley.
✓ Oops! Zorb flies through a meteor shower.
✓ Get a new glow at the Antenna Shine Shop.
✓ Stop at the garage to pound out the dents from the meteor shower.

ANSWER ON PAGE 75

We Gave It a Swirl

Use the clues below to figure out which animals appear in these swirled pictures. ANSWERS ON PAGE 75

1

HINT: This skilled hunter has really earned its stripes.

2

HINT: Just call this animal Spot.

3

HINT: Don't mistake these funny-looking friends for penguins.

4

HINT: Make eye contact with this rain forest creature and you'll be seeing red.

5

HINT: This type of insect has a name similar to a famous rock band's name.

Just for Kicks

Have you been in a game like this one? The seven circles below are parts of this crazy scene. Circle the spot where each part comes from. ANSWERS ON PAGE 75

Trading
Places

These animals got mixed up! They are all in the wrong habitats. Write each animal's name (listed below) in the space beside its correct habitat name.

ANSWERS ON PAGE 75

- orangutan
- camel
- brown bear
- bullfrog
- clown fish
- giraffe
- emperor penguin

1 **Pond** North America

bullfrog

2 **Savanna** Africa

giraffe

3 **Desert** Africa — Camel

5 **Ocean** Antarctica — emporer penguin

6 **Rain Forest** Asia — oranitang

4 **Coral Reef** Australia — Clown fish

7 **Tundra** North America — Brown bear

WILD GUESS

Compare these pairs, if you dare.

ANSWERS ON PAGE 75

1 Which is taller?

giraffe ⟷ T. rex

2 Which takes longer?

popping microwave popcorn — a ride on the world's longest roller coaster

4 Which sound travels farther?

a lion's roar — thunder

3 Which is heavier?

space shuttle — Leaning Tower of Pisa

5 Which is faster?

the fastest racehorse — the fastest baseball pitch

6 Which is bigger?

MAPS NOT TO SCALE

California — Italy

It's a Jungle Out There!

START

DO NOT DISTURB

MAN-EATING PLANTS

DANGER QUICKSAND

SWIM at your own risk

BARREL OF MONKEYS

FINISH

Help this explorer make her way safely to this tree house. Only one path is danger free!
ANSWER ON PAGE 75

What in the World?

Play interactive "What in the World?" and other games online. kids.nationalgeographic.com

ALOHA SPIRIT

These photographs show close-up and faraway views of things you could see in Hawaii. Unscramble the letters to identify what's in each picture. ANSWERS ON PAGE 75

EPPIEPLSNA

SELI

TOCNCOU

AIWAAHIN SIRHT

ESA REUTLT

NVLAOOC

DAUSRFOBR

EKUULLE

Surprises in the Teachers' LOUNGE

Someone played a prank in the teachers' lounge by switching the labels on ten items. Can you figure out which labels belong on the objects listed below? Write the letter for the correct label beside the name of each object.

ANSWERS ON PAGE 75

1. Superman suit ___ E
2. eyeglasses ___
3. hairspray ___
4. balloons ___
5. eggs ___
6. ice pop ___
7. bike mirror ___
8. dog food ___
9. TV dinner ___
10. orange juice ___

Funny FILL-IN
Running Wild!

Ask someone to give you words to fill in the blanks in this story without showing it to him or her. Then read it out loud for a laugh.

My pet __Snake__ is always getting into trouble. His name is __Yogi__, and all of the neighbors
(type of animal) _(cartoon character)_

know him. Most days you can find him chewing on __Mathew__'s __gold__. But I don't
(your neighbor's name) _(something valuable)_

know what got into him yesterday. I had just taken him out for his morning __run__ when a(n)
(noun)

__Dragon__ leaped out from behind a(n) __house__. __yogio__ jumped __1000__ feet
(animal) _(large object)_ _(same cartoon character)_ _(large number)_

in the air! Then his __Stuffed anml__ puffed up, and he started to __Rore__ really loudly.
(something soft) _(sound made by an animal)_

He took off __running__ at about __100000__ miles an hour. Luckily he had stepped in
(verb ending in –ing) _(large number)_

__a poppydiper__ and left a trail of __Dirty__ __tail__ prints all the way to the nearest
(something mushy) _(adjective)_ _(animal body part)_

__Toys-R-us__. By the time I got there, three __Preaty__ employees were chasing my __ugley__
(name of a store) _(adjective)_ _(adjective)_

pet out of the store. The animal was __running__ down the street with a brand-new pair of
(action verb ending in –ing)

__Nikes__ on his __Paw__. The next thing I knew, he dashed into __chickfolau__, jumped
(popular sneakers) _(animal body part)_ _(name of a restaurant)_

onto a(n) __Couch__, snatched __Hambergers__ off a customer's plate, and ran out the back door. I
(furniture) _(food, plural)_

thought I had lost him completely when I walked by __Target__. There he was, curled up asleep next to
(another store)

a(n) __aligator__ in the window. As __Happiley__ as I could, I clipped on his __house__ and
(different animal) _(adverb ending in –ly)_ _(noun)_

walked him straight to my __Washrater__. Boy, was he in the __Tiger__ house!
(building monument) _(animal)_

BISTRO

City Gone WILD!

Wild animals have moved into the big city, and they're fitting in a little too well. Find and circle ten wild animals hiding in this scene. Look carefully—you might see them in some funny places.

ANSWERS ON PAGE 75

READ BETWEEN THE LINES

These drawings aren't just doodles! Match each drawing with its title listed below. Write the correct letters in the spaces provided.

ANSWERS ON PAGE 75

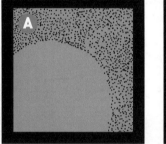

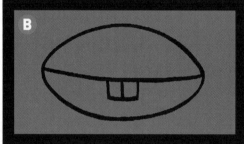

1. Worm Taking a Date to Dinner ____
2. Clam with Buckteeth ____
3. Germs Avoiding Friend Who Has Caught Antibiotics ____
4. Tennis Ball (Factory Reject) ____
5. Man Playing Trombone in a Phone Booth ____
6. Snake Going Up Stairs ____
7. Tall Cow ____
8. Rich Sardine with Private Can ____
9. Bubble Gum Champ ____
10. Four Elephants Inspecting a Grapefruit ____

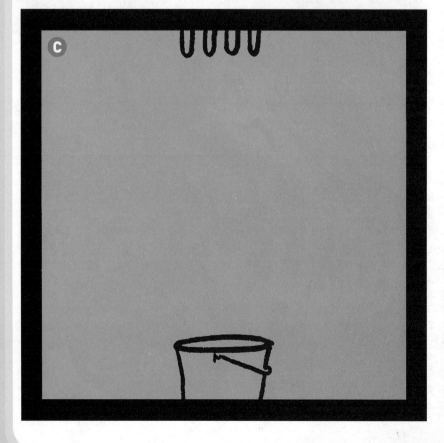

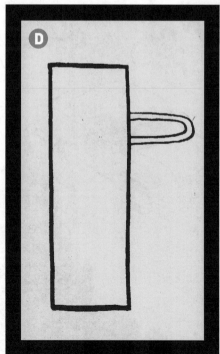

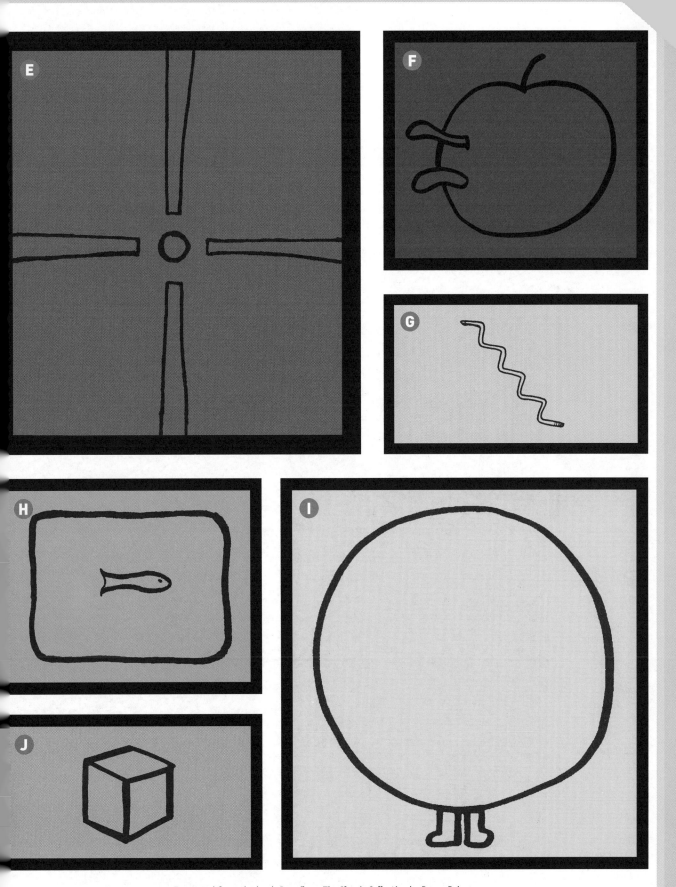

Excerpted from the book *Droodles—The Classic Collection* by Roger Price.

EYE ★ MAGIC

Hold this image to your nose and pretend you're looking through it. Without refocusing or blinking, slowly move it away from you. The jumble of blurry images suddenly turns into one 3-D picture! Although this tricky pic was created on a computer, the concept—called a stereogram—has been around for decades. The image gives your left eye and your right eye different views. Your brain then puts the two views together. The result is three bugs on a computer: computer bugs! ANSWER ON PAGE 76

One complete blink takes about a third of a second.

The average person blinks automatically every four to six seconds.

It's OK if you can't see this illusion. Not everyone can!

PET PROJECT

Ten people in this store will each take home a new pet today. Using clues in the picture, match the ten people to their future pets. Then draw lines connecting the pairs.

ANSWERS ON PAGE 76

Find the HIDDEN ANIMALS

Animals often blend into their environments for protection. Find each animal listed below in one of the pictures. Write the letter of the correct picture next to each animal's name.

ANSWERS ON PAGE 76

1. jaguar   ~~C~~
2. fish   ~~A~~
3. arctic fox   ~~A~~
4. shrimp   ___
5. caterpillar   ___
6. seahorse   ___
7. crab   ___
8. sea snake   ___
9. katydid   ___
10. moth   ___
11. chameleon   ___

B SCOTLAND

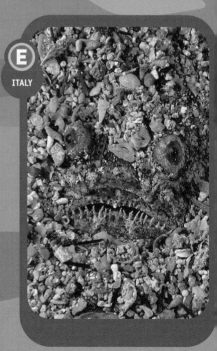

D SPAIN

C NORTHERN IRELAND

E ITALY

A INDONESIA

F
COSTA
RICA

I
INDONESIA

G
BRAZIL

J
JAPAN

H
CANADA

K
INDONESIA

Take the Plunge

Help this scuba diver clean up the coral reef. Find the following items that don't belong under the sea:

- toy car
- in-line skate
- wristwatch
- peanut butter
- beach ball
- sneaker
- sunglasses
- bananas
- suntan lotion
- scooter
- boat oar

ANSWERS ON PAGE 76

STUMP
YOUR PARENTS

If your parents can't answer these questions, maybe *they* should go to school instead of you!

ANSWERS ON PAGE 76

1 What was the R.M.S. *Titanic*'s final destination before it sank in 1912?
A. Boston, Massachusetts
B. New York City, New York
C. Halifax, Nova Scotia, in Canada
D. Philadelphia, Pennsylvania

2 If you were a gladiator in ancient Rome, who would you most likely fight?
A. professional fighter
B. criminal
C. slave
D. all of the above

3 In *Pirates of the Caribbean: At World's End*, which mythological monster is found dead on the beach after Captain Jack Sparrow is rescued from Davy Jones's Locker?
A. a kraken
B. a dragon
C. a cyclops
D. an ogre

4 Which of these was recently reclassified as a dwarf planet?
A. Mercury
B. Neptune
C. Saturn
D. Uranus
E. Jupiter
F. Pluto
G. Earth
H. Mars

5 Which Springfield is where the Simpsons live?
A. Springfield, Massachusetts
B. Springfield, Missouri
C. Springfield, Illinois
D. none of the above

6 Which superhero is based in a real place?
A. Batman/Gotham City
B. Superman/Metropolis
C. Wolverine/Westchester County, New York
D. Buffy the Vampire Slayer/ Sunnydale, California

7 Which theme park does not have a site in Florida, in the U.S.A.?
A. Magic Kingdom
B. Six Flags
C. SeaWorld
D. Universal Studios

8 Which vacation destination is the oldest?
A. Grand Canyon, in the United States
B. Pyramids at Giza, in Egypt
C. London, England, in the United Kingdom
D. Great Wall of China

9 Lions do *not* live in which habitat?
A. desert
B. savanna
C. rain forest
D. forest

Perfect Match

Nine sets of identical twins and one set of triplets go to Camp Double Take. Find the look-alike(s) for each numbered camper. Hint: The clothing for the correct matches is identical, but some of the kids are wearing different sports gear. ANSWERS ON PAGE 76

GIRLS' SHOWERS

SEEING SPOTS

Play interactive "What in the World?" and other games online. nationalgeographic.com/ngkids

These photographs are close-up views of things with spots or dots. Unscramble the letters to identify each picture. Feel like you're on the spot? ANSWERS ON PAGE 76

SWRTITE

HERAFTE

COGEK

YAGBDLU

lady bug

MDOOIN

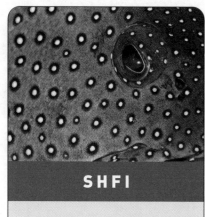

SHFI

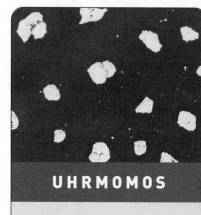

AYDNC TSBTONU

UHRMOMOS

Ask someone to give you words to fill in the blanks in this story without showing it to him or her. Then read it out loud for a laugh.

Reporter: Good evening. This is _Abraamlinkin_ reporting to you live from _Lexington lane_,
famous person / a street in your town

where _Peter sire_ claims to have spotted a mysterious creature in _windmill hill park_.
friend's full name, male / a park in your town

I have Mr. _Sire_ here to tell us what he saw.
same friend's last name

Friend: I was _running_ on that _butterfly_ right over there when I heard a(n)
action verb ending in -ing / noun

walking in the _lakes_. Then I heard a(n) _squek_. Before I knew
verb ending in -ing / object in nature, plural / animal noise

it, a _Elephent_ appeared. It looked like it was half _butterfly_ and half _cow_. It had
something huge / noun / animal

_6_ _arms_ and a coat of _blue_ _pillows_. Then it disappeared into
number / body part, plural / color / something soft, plural

the _Snakes_. I have pictures right here in my _computer_. Take a look!
object in nature, plural / high-tech gadget

Reporter: _Run_! That really is something. It looks like you placed a(n)
exclamation

Mickey mouse doll on top of a(n) _geraf_ and hid it in the woods.
movie character / something tall

Friend: You don't have to believe me, but I know I saw the _Unicorn_!
mysterious creature

Reporter: Well, viewers, you heard it straight from the _kitty_'s mouth. Now back to the studio,
animal

where _Donald Duck_ discusses his new reality TV show *'Toon Life*.
male cartoon character

1

2

3

SIGNS
OF THE TIMES

**Think seeing is believing? Not always!
Two of these signs are not real.
Can you figure out which
ones are fake?**

ANSWERS ON
PAGE 76

4

NEXT 96 km

ALIEN PARKING

5

6

WATCH FOR ICE

7

Teeing Off

Find at least 30 items on this miniature golf course that start with the letter *t*.
ANSWERS ON PAGE 76

Lost in Spa

The Moon Rock concert just ended, but now these aliens can't find their spaceships in the parking lot. To help each alien locate its spaceship, follow these rules:

- Aliens with antennae need ships with pointed roofs.
- Short aliens need ladders to reach the doors of their ships.
- The number of windows on the spaceship must match the number of eyeballs on the alien.
- Purple aliens must return to the Purple Planet in purple spaceships.

ANSWERS ON PAGE 76

The Funnies

"UM...MY OWNER ATE MY HOMEWORK."

"NOT EVERYONE'S A DOG PERSON!"

"DO YOU HAVE ANY IDEA HOW FAST YOU WERE GOING BACK THERE?"

Having a Blast!

These expressions describe guests at this barbecue—literally! Find and circle the people in the scene who match these descriptions.

1. Joe is all ears.
2. Brittany is a barrel of laughs.
3. Gretchen bends over backward for her friends.
4. John is good at breaking the ice.
5. Jane is a backseat driver.
6. Peter just opened a can of worms.
7. Kaitlyn is getting married in two days and has cold feet.
8. Brandon is ready to hit the sack.
9. Emily is in the doghouse.
10. Jake just let the cat out of the bag. ANSWERS ON PAGE 77

GO FISH!

Something's fishy at this aquarium. Find and circle the following items that are hidden in this scene.

surfboard
cowboy hat
sunflower
wrapped gift
bike wheel
teacup and saucer
plate of spaghetti
soft pretzel
guitar

ANSWERS ON PAGE 77

We Gave It a Swirl

Use the clues below to figure out which animals appear in these swirled pictures. ANSWERS ON PAGE 77

1

HINT! A movie starring this clown did swimmingly at the box office.

2

HINT! If this sprinter took off down a highway, it could run fast enough to get a speeding ticket.

3

HINT! Hey, who are you calling a quack?

4

HINT! Slowing down climate change can help protect animals like this Arctic giant.

5

HINT! This many-legged creature will go through a major transformation.

Wild and Wacky ROAD TRIP
U.S.A.

Ruby Slippers
Oz, Kansas

T. Rex
Cabazon, California

P

Two of these giant roadside attractions are *not* real. Can you guess which ones are fake? ANSWERS ON PAGE 77

PB and J
Sandwich, Georgia

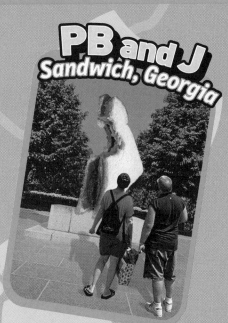

World's Largest Egg
Winlock, Washington

World's Largest EGG

Paul Bunyan
Akeley, Minnesota

Carhenge
Alliance, Nebraska

SPLASH DOWN

START!

enter

Slide your way through this water park without splashing down into the wrong pool. You want to end up in the big wave pool to meet up with your friends.

ANSWER ON PAGE 77

Name That ANIMAL

Many dog and cat breeds are named after different countries. Can you match the international names below with these pets? Write the correct letter next to each animal name below.

ANSWERS ON PAGE 77

1. Russian blue
2. English setter
3. Siamese cat (Siam is now called Thailand.)
4. Afghan hound
5. French bulldog
6. Persian cat (Persia is now called Iran.)
7. English cocker spaniel
8. German shepherd
9. Irish setter
10. Italian greyhound

The River Wild

LAUNCH

TAKE-OUT

Steer this raft safely from the LAUNCH to the TAKE-OUT site. Only one route offers thrills and avoids spills and chills! ANSWER ON PAGE 77

The Funnies

"PLAID IS THE NEW STRIPES!"

ANIMALS THAT YOU MIGHT RUN INTO AT SCHOOL.

"YOU'VE GOT FOOD STUCK IN YOUR TEETH AGAIN!"

A Piece of Cake

Find at least 25 items in this bakery that start with the letter *b*. ANSWERS ON PAGE 77

Make a SPLASH!

Many expressions don't mean what they say. For example, if you have butterflies in your stomach, that really means you're nervous. This swimming pool scene shows ten expressions exactly as they are worded. For example, number one is "pie in the sky." Can you figure out which expression appears in each of the numbered pictures?
ANSWERS ON PAGE 77

What in the World?

Play interactive "What in the World?" and other games online. kids.nationalgeographic.com

FACE-TO-FACE

These faces aren't staring you down—they're familiar items seen from odd angles. Unscramble the letters to unmask their identities. ANSWERS ON PAGE 77

NSGPOHPI ABG

ECTSH FO RSDWAER

ALWL KTSCOE

RLEWFO

flower

SIGFHNI ATH

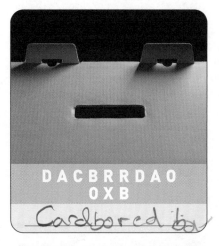

DACBRRDAO OXB

Cardbored box

UCP DLI

cup lid

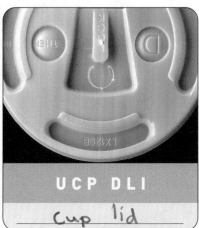

LMBRAE EACK

POM

MoP

47

Lost and Found

These moviegoers have lost their belongings. Find these missing items in the movie theater lobby.

ANSWERS ON PAGE 77

- bag of popcorn
- hot dog
- water bottle
- soft pretzel
- ice-cream cone
- peanuts
- movie ticket
- backpack
- cell phone
- sunglasses
- umbrella
- iPod

SIGNS
OF THE TIMES

Can you figure out which two of these
signs are fake?

ANSWERS
ON PAGE 78

1

2

HAM
SANDWICH 3 ½

FINGLESHAM EASTRY R.D.C.

3

SOFT
SHOULDER

4

CornDog 00 LN

5

READLYN
"857 friendly people
AND ONE OLD GRUMP"

6

NO
TURNS
8ᴬᴹ – 7ᵀᴴ
EXCEPT SUNDAY

DONT
LOOK

7

NO
WAY

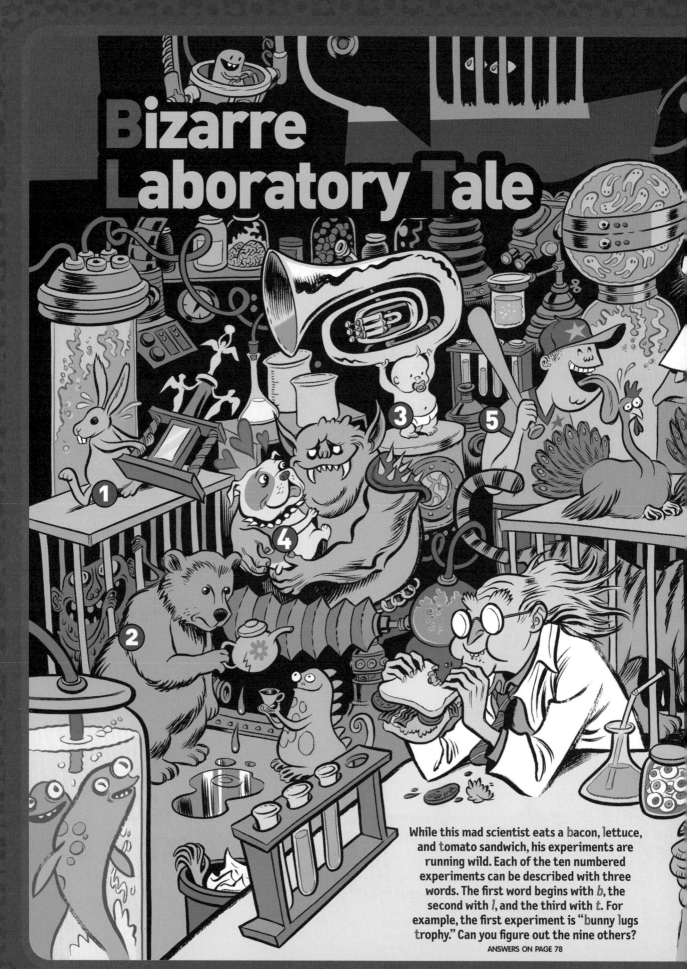

Bizarre Laboratory Tale

While this mad scientist eats a **b**acon, **l**ettuce, and **t**omato sandwich, his experiments are running wild. Each of the ten numbered experiments can be described with three words. The first word begins with *b*, the second with *l*, and the third with *t*. For example, the first experiment is "**b**unny **l**ugs **t**rophy." Can you figure out the nine others?

ANSWERS ON PAGE 78

Mousetrap

A tiny mouse has sneaked into this restaurant and caused chaos. Find 20 things in the dining room that the mouse has nibbled on, and then find the mouse. We've circled one nibble for you.
ANSWERS ON PAGE 78

Name That Animal!

2 _____ Spider monkey

1 _____ Ty

Imagine what a catfish would look like if it were really part cat and part fish. These pictures show how other animals with combination names might appear if they looked exactly like their names. Fill in the correct name of each animal. For example, the first one is part tiger and part shark, so the answer is tiger shark.   ANSWERS ON PAGE 78

5 _____

4 _____ dragonfly

3 _____ bullfrog

6 _____ zebrafish

April Showers

A spring rain isn't the only surprise in this town square. Find and circle at least ten things that are wrong in this scene. ANSWERS ON PAGE 78

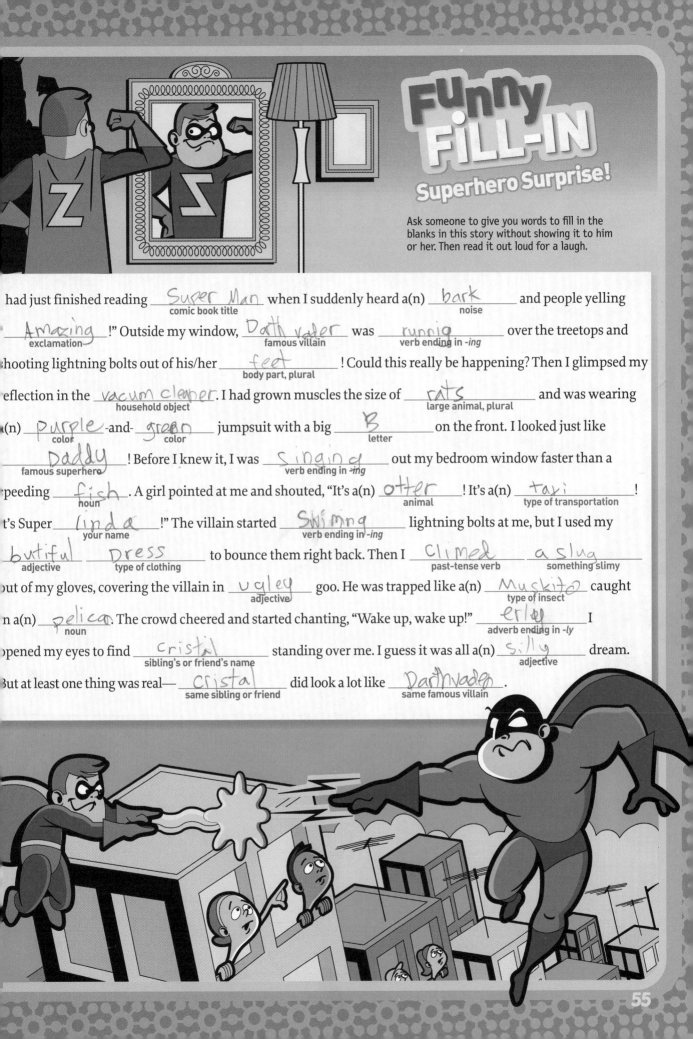

Funny Fill-IN
Superhero Surprise!

Ask someone to give you words to fill in the blanks in this story without showing it to him or her. Then read it out loud for a laugh.

had just finished reading __Super Man__ (comic book title) when I suddenly heard a(n) __bark__ (noise) and people yelling

"__Amazing__ (exclamation)!" Outside my window, __Darth vader__ (famous villain) was __runnig__ (verb ending in -ing) over the treetops and

shooting lightning bolts out of his/her __feet__ (body part, plural)! Could this really be happening? Then I glimpsed my

reflection in the __vacum claner__ (household object). I had grown muscles the size of __rats__ (large animal, plural) and was wearing

a(n) __purple__ (color)-and-__green__ (color) jumpsuit with a big __B__ (letter) on the front. I looked just like

__Daddy__ (famous superhero)! Before I knew it, I was __singing__ (verb ending in -ing) out my bedroom window faster than a

speeding __fish__ (noun). A girl pointed at me and shouted, "It's a(n) __otter__ (animal)! It's a(n) __taxi__ (type of transportation)!

It's Super__linda__ (your name)!" The villain started __swiming__ (verb ending in -ing) lightning bolts at me, but I used my

__butiful__ (adjective) __Dress__ (type of clothing) to bounce them right back. Then I __climed__ (past-tense verb) __a slug__ (something slimy)

out of my gloves, covering the villain in __ugley__ (adjective) goo. He was trapped like a(n) __Muskito__ (type of insect) caught

in a(n) __pelica__ (noun). The crowd cheered and started chanting, "Wake up, wake up!" __erlly__ (adverb ending in -ly) I

opened my eyes to find __cristal__ (sibling's or friend's name) standing over me. I guess it was all a(n) __silly__ (adjective) dream.

But at least one thing was real— __cristal__ (same sibling or friend) did look a lot like __Darthvader__ (same famous villain).

55

Beach Bound

Bob.B

DETOUR

GASOLINE
REGULAR

Bigfoot
X-ing

Road
Closed

Aunt Bertha wants to have some fun in the sun! Help her find the only route to the beach. ANSWER ON PAGE 78

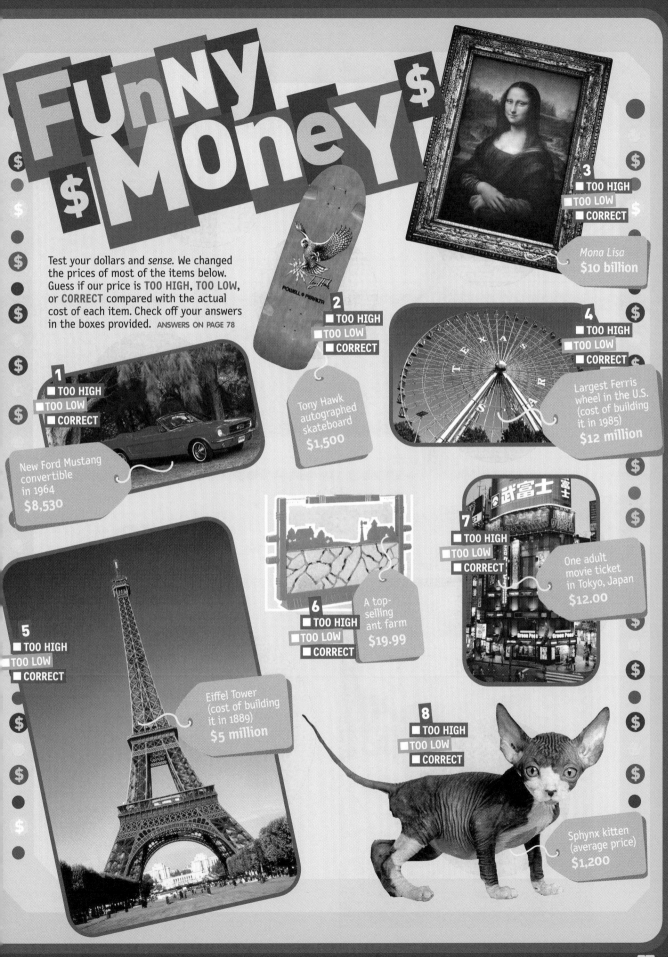

Funny $Money$

Test your dollars and *sense*. We changed the prices of most of the items below. Guess if our price is **TOO HIGH**, **TOO LOW**, or **CORRECT** compared with the actual cost of each item. Check off your answers in the boxes provided. ANSWERS ON PAGE 78

3
- ■ TOO HIGH
- ■ TOO LOW
- ■ CORRECT

Mona Lisa
$10 billion

2
- ■ TOO HIGH
- ■ TOO LOW
- ■ CORRECT

Tony Hawk autographed skateboard
$1,500

4
- ■ TOO HIGH
- ■ TOO LOW
- ■ CORRECT

Largest Ferris wheel in the U.S. (cost of building it in 1985)
$12 million

1
- ■ TOO HIGH
- ■ TOO LOW
- ■ CORRECT

New Ford Mustang convertible in 1964
$8,530

7
- ■ TOO HIGH
- ■ TOO LOW
- ■ CORRECT

One adult movie ticket in Tokyo, Japan
$12.00

6
- ■ TOO HIGH
- ■ TOO LOW
- ■ CORRECT

A top-selling ant farm **$19.99**

5
- ■ TOO HIGH
- ■ TOO LOW
- ■ CORRECT

Eiffel Tower (cost of building it in 1889)
$5 million

8
- ■ TOO HIGH
- ■ TOO LOW
- ■ CORRECT

Sphynx kitten (average price)
$1,200

Spaced-OUT

Each box below contains a term that's related to outer space. Figure out each one by looking closely at the way it is shown here. Then write it in the space provided. We've done the first one for you. ANSWERS ON PAGE 78

1 BLACK HOLE

2 TERRESTRIAL TERRESTRIAL

3 YEAR

4 METEOR

5 STAR

6 DIPPER

The Funnies

"THEY'RE SURPRISINGLY EASY TO TRAIN!"

Change of Heart

Love is in the air on this city street, and it has everyone turned around. All of these small scenes are upside-down or sideways. Find each small scene in the big picture. ANSWERS ON PAGE 78

We Gave It a Swirl

Use the clues below to figure out which animals appear in these swirled pictures. ANSWERS ON PAGE 78

1 HINT! Pink never goes out of style for this leggy creature.

2 HINT! These teddy bear look-alikes aren't really bears.

3 HINT! This gentle giant likes to *moo*-ve in a herd.

4 HINT! Falsely known as a master of camouflage, this animal may actually change color to communicate, not to blend in.

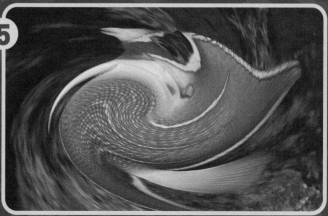

5 HINT: This animal doesn't mind spending its entire life in a school.

Funny FiLL-IN

A Royal Vacation

Ask someone to give you words to fill in the blanks in this story without showing it to him or her. Then read out it loud for a laugh.

SCREEEEECH!

This summer my family and I took a(n) __fun__ (adjective) trip to London, England. After a(n) __1__ (number) -hour flight, we found out that the airline lost our __bags__ (plural noun). So I ended up wearing the same __justin timberlake__ (popular singer) T-shirt for the whole trip! On the way to the hotel, I was staring out the car window when I saw a(n) __gold__ (color) double-decker __backpack__ (noun) coming right at us! My dad had forgotten that the British __run__ (verb) on the __brown__ (adjective) side of the road! He shouted, "__flowers__ (exclamation)!" and then __played__ (past-tense verb) onto the sidewalk in front of __Sanders__ (your neighbor's last name) Palace—the home of __Alex morgan__ (famous female person). Luckily no one at the __exited__ (adjective) palace seemed to notice. Everyone was __running__ (verb ending in -ing) in the opposite direction. I jumped up and down to see over them when my foot __loved__ (past-tense verb) on a piece of __pasta__ (food), I hit my __leg__ (body part) on a(n) __Donut__ (noun), and then everything went __blue__ (color). The next thing I knew, __Alex morgan__ (same famous female as above) was helping me up and inviting me to the __White house__ (famous place) for dinner. She was throwing a party, and the guest of honor was __Justin timberlake__ (same singer as above)!

GO UNDERCOVER!

These photos show close-up views of animals you may recognize. To identify them, unscramble the letters below each picture. ANSWERS ON PAGE 79

WACAM
_____

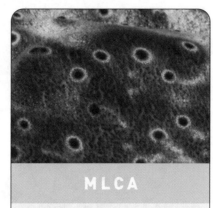

MLCA
_____

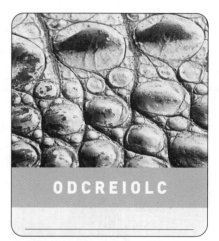

ODCREIOLC
_____

UJRAGA
_____

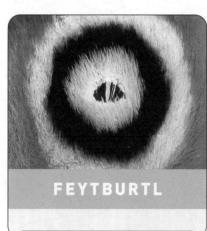

FEYTBURTL
_____

REZBA
_____

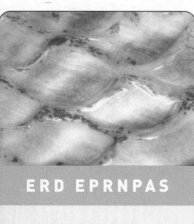

ERD EPRNPAS
_____

EFRAGIF
_____

OLMHACEEN
_____

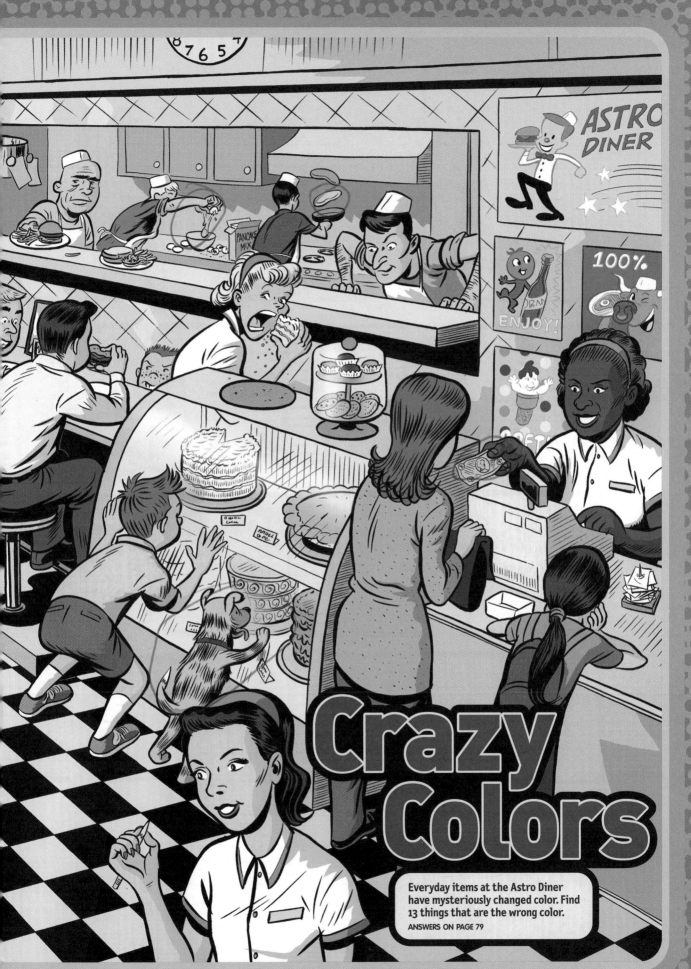

Crazy Colors

Everyday items at the Astro Diner have mysteriously changed color. Find 13 things that are the wrong color.

ANSWERS ON PAGE 79

SCHOOL DAZE

Jake's science experiment ended with a bang. Now he's late for gym class, and he still has errands to do. Find the route that will get him from the science lab to the stops on his list in order. He can't walk along the same route twice and can't pass the entrances to the teachers' lounge and principal's office. **HINTS: You must pass the entrance to each room on the list. And you must use the stairs to move between floors.** ANSWERS ON PAGE 79

TO DO:
1. Return book to library
2. Stop by locker
3. Visit Joe in cafeteria
4. Go to gym class

Lucky PENny

Here's a real eye-oPENer! The name of each of the numbered items on this page contains the word *pen*. Are you lucky enough to be able to name each item?

ANSWERS ON PAGE 79

STATE

PeneaPasta

Pencils

IN CONGRESS,
us Declaration of the thirteen united Sta

The Funnies

"MY DOG DELETED MY HOMEWORK FROM MY HARD DRIVE!"

"THANKS, MOM. BUT CAN I SUPERSIZE THAT?"

"KIDS THESE DAYS...ALWAYS LOOKING FOR THE EASY WAY OUT!"

BIG AIR!

What's it like to see through someone else's eyes? The small views at the bottom of this page show what seven kids at this skate park see from where they are positioned. Match each view to the correct kid. ANSWERS ON PAGE 79

Ski Patrol

Be on the lookout for things that are out of place at this ski resort. Find and circle at least 15 wrong items in this scene. ANSWERS ON PAGE 79

SKI RENTALS

SKEE SKOOL

We Gave It a Swirl

Use the clues below to figure out which animals appear in these swirled pictures.

ANSWERS ON PAGE 79

1

HINT!
What's black and white and furry all over?

2

HINT!
There are plenty of these in the sea.

3

HINT!
This critter has scales and a long tail.

Picnic PUZZLER

Each box below illustrates a term that's related to a picnic. Figure out each one by looking closely at the way it is shown here, and then write the term in the space below it. We've done the first one for you.

ANSWERS ON PAGE 79

1

ANTHILL

2

3

4

5

6

71

TREASURE HUNT

This explorer has discovered an ancient city in the jungle. Help her find these items hidden in this secret world.

ANSWERS ON PAGE 79

1. diamonds
2. gold coins
3. monkey statue
4. rock art
5. bow and arrow
6. treasure map
7. treasure chest
8. crown
9. drum
10. cave opening

DANGER! QUICKSAND!

Bowling Freeze-Frame

BFF doesn't stand for only "best friends forever." Can you figure out the three-word phrase that describes each of the numbered scenes in this bowling alley? The first word always begins with *b*, and the second and third words always begin with *f*. For example, the answer to number one is "**B**aboon **f**ries **f**ish."

ANSWERS ON PAGE 79

Answers

Out of This World, pages 6–7

We Gave It a Swirl, page 8

1. TIGER, 2. DALMATION, 3. PUFFIN, 4. RED-EYED TREE FROG, 5. BEETLE.

Just for Kicks, page 9

Trading Places, pages 10–11

1. BULLFROG, 2. GIRAFFE, 3. CAMEL, 4. CLOWN FISH, 5. EMPEROR PENGUIN, 6. ORANGUTAN, 7. BROWN BEAR.

Wild Guess, page 12

1. AN ADULT T-REX STOOD UP TO 20 FEET TALL; ADULT GIRAFFES STAND UP TO 19 FEET TALL. 2. RIDING THE 8,133-FOOT-LONG STEEL DRAGON ROLLER COASTER IN JAPAN TOOK 3 MINUTES, 40 SECONDS; MICROWAVE POPCORN COOKS FOR AN AVERAGE OF TWO TO THREE MINUTES. 3.THE LEANING TOWER OF PISA WEIGHS ABOUT 31.9 MILLION POUNDS; THE SPACE SHUTTLE WEIGHS ABOUT 4.4 MILLION POUNDS. 4. THUNDER CAN BE HEARD UP TO 12 MILES AWAY; A LION'S ROAR CAN BE HEARD 5 MILES AWAY. 5. THE FASTEST BASEBALL PITCH REACHED 107.9 MILES AN HOUR; THE FASTEST RACEHORSE RAN 45 MILES AN HOUR. 6. CALIFORNIA IS 158,706 SQUARE MILES; ITALY IS 116,000 SQUARE MILES.

It's a Jungle Out There!, page 13

What in the World?: Aloha Spirit, page 14

TOP ROW: PINEAPPLES, LEIS, COCONUT.
MIDDLE ROW: HAWAIIAN SHIRT, HULA DANCER DOLL, SEA TURTLE.
BOTTOM ROW: VOLCANO, SURFBOARD, UKULELE.

Surprises in the Teachers' Lounge, page 15

1. E, 2. A, 3. I, 4. J, 5. H, 6. C, 7. D, 8. F, 9. G, 10. B.

City Gone Wild!, page 17

Read Between the Lines, pages 18–19

1. F, 2. B, 3. A, 4. J, 5. D, 6. G, 7. C, 8. H, 9. I, 10. E.

Eye Magic, page 20

© 2010 Magic Eye Inc.

Pet Project, page 21

Find the Hidden Animals, pages 22–23

1. G, 2. E, 3. H, 4. A, 5. B, 6. I, 7. J, 8. K, 9. F, 10. C, 11. D.

Take the Plunge, page 24

Stump Your Parents, page 25

1. B; 2. D; 3. A; 4. F; 5. D (THE SHOW HAS NEVER REVEALED WHICH STATE THE SIMPSONS LIVE IN).; 6. C; 7. B; 8. A; 9. C.

Perfect Match, pages 26–27

What in the World?: Seeing Spots, page 28

TOP ROW: TWISTER, FEATHER, GECKO. **MIDDLE ROW:** LADYBUG, DALMATIAN, DOMINO. **BOTTOM ROW:** FISH, CANDY BUTTONS, MUSHROOM.

Signs of the Times, page 30

SIGNS #2 AND #6 ARE FAKE.

Teeing Off, page 31

(FROM TOP TO BOTTOM, LEFT TO RIGHT): TAJ MAHAL, TOWEL, TENT, TOWER OF PISA, TRAIN TRACKS, TRAIN, TOTEM POLE, TRASH CAN, TOOLBOX, T-SHIRT, TROMBONE, TIE, TABLES, TACOS, TOMATOES, TELEPHONE BOOTH, TEDDY BEAR, TRAMPOLINE, "THE END" SIGN, TONGUE, TRUCK, TIRES, TICKETS, TOUCAN, TEETH, TURTLE, TULIPS, TREES, TENNIS RACKET, TEES.

Lost in Space, pages 32-33

1. G, 2. C, 3. F, 4. B, 5. D, 6. E, 7. A.

Having a Blast!, page 35

Go Fish!, page 36

We Gave It a Swirl, page 37
1. CLOWN FISH, 2. CHEETAH, 3. DUCKLING, 4. POLAR BEAR, 5. CATERPILLAR.

Wild and Wacky Road Trip U.S.A., pages 38–39
PB AND J AND RUBY SLIPPERS ARE FAKE.

Splash Down, pages 40–41

Name That Animal, page 42
1. D, 2. H, 3. E, 4. C, 5. F, 6. I, 7. B, 8. G, 9. J, 10. A.

The River Wild, page 43

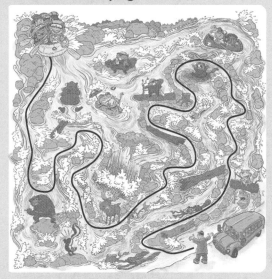

A Piece of Cake, page 45
(FROM LEFT TO RIGHT, TOP TO BOTTOM): BOY, BIRTHDAY CAKE, BULLDOG, BICYCLE, BUBBLES, BREAD, BARREL, BALL, BROOM, BERET, BOOK, BEAR, BELT, BUNS, BALLERINA, BALLOONS, BOX, BOW TIE, BONES, BASKET, BUTTONS, BAGELS, BAKER, BOWL, BUTTER.

Make a Splash!, page 46
1. PIE IN THE SKY, 2. RAINING CATS AND DOGS, 3. OUT ON A LIMB, 4. PULLING YOUR LEG, 5. WATER UNDER THE BRIDGE, 6. GET YOUR DUCKS IN A ROW, 7. FLY ON THE WALL, 8. BITE OFF MORE THAN YOU CAN CHEW, 9. ANTS IN YOUR PANTS, 10. CAT'S GOT YOUR TONGUE.

What in the World?: Face-to-Face, page 47
TOP ROW: SHOPPING BAG, CHEST OF DRAWERS, WALL SOCKET.
MIDDLE ROW: FLOWER, FISHING HAT, CARDBOARD BOX.
BOTTOM ROW: CUP LID, MARBLE CAKE, MOP.

Lost and Found, page 48

Signs of the Times, page 49
SIGNS #1 AND #6 ARE FAKE.

Bizarre Laboratory Tale, pages 50–51
1. BUNNY LUGS TROPHY, 2. BEAR LEAKS TEA, 3. BABY LIFTS TUBA,
4. BULLDOG LOVES TROLL, 5. BATTER LICKS TURKEY, 6. BLACK BELT LIGHTS
TORCH, 7. BEAVER LOCKS TIGER, 8. BOXER LOSES TIC-TAC-TOE,
9. BALLERINA LASSOS TUT, 10. BRIDE LEADS TWINS.

Mousetrap, page 52

Name That Animal!, page 53
1. TIGER SHARK, 2. SPIDER MONKEY, 3. BULLFROG, 4. DRAGONFLY,
5. ELEPHANT SEAL, 6. ZEBRA FISH.

April Showers, page 54

Beach Bound, page 56
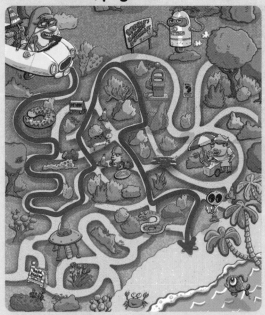

Funny Money, page 57
1. TOO HIGH. REAL PRICE: $2,614; 2. TOO LOW. REAL PRICE: $6,000; 3. TOO
LOW. THE *MONA LISA* IS PRICELESS. 4. TOO HIGH. REAL PRICE: $2.2 MIL-
LION; 5. TOO HIGH. REAL PRICE: $1.56 MILLION; 6. TOO HIGH. REAL PRICE:
$9.99; 7. TOO LOW. REAL PRICE: $15.15 (AVERAGE); 8. CORRECT.

Spaced-Out, page 58
1. BLACK HOLE, 2. EXTRATERRESTRIAL, 3. LIGHT-YEAR, 4. METEOR SHOWER,
5. SHOOTING STAR, 6. LITTLE DIPPER

Change of Heart, page 59

Save Our Ship!, page 60
1. SAILOR OPERATES SAW, 2. SHOPKEEPER ORGANIZES SUNSCREEN,
3. SEAGULLS OVERLOAD SAILBOAT, 4. SWIMMER OFFERS SANDWICH,
5. SHEEPDOG OBEYS SURFER, 6. SOLDIER OPENS SAFE, 7. SNORKELER
ORDERS SUNDAE.

We Gave It a Swirl, page 61
1. PINK FLAMINGO, 2. KOALA, 3. COW, 4. CHAMELEON, 5. FISH.

What in the World?, page 63

TOP ROW: MACAW, CLAM, CROCODILE. **MIDDLE ROW:** JAGUAR, BUTTERFLY, ZEBRA. **BOTTOM ROW:** RED SNAPPER, GIRAFFE, CHAMELEON.

Crazy Colors, pages 64–65

School Daze, page 66

Lucky PENny, page 67

1. PENNY, 2. PENNANT, 3. PENNE PASTA, 4. PENDULUM, 5. COLORED PENCILS, 6. DECLARATION OF INDEPENDENCE, 7. CARPENTER, 8. PENGUIN, 9. PENINSULA, 10. CAN OPENER, 11. PENDANT, 12. PENCIL SHARPENER, 13. PIGPEN.

Big Air!, page 69

Ski Patrol, page 70

We Gave It a Swirl, page 71

1. PANDA, 2. FISH, 3. IGUANA.

Picnic Puzzler, page 71

1. ANTHILL, 2. ICED TEA, 3. HOT DOG, 4. KETCHUP, 5. TOSSED SALAD, 6. BACKYARD.

Treasure Hunt, pages 72–73

Bowling Freeze-Frame, page 74

1. BABOON FRIES FISH, 2. BOY FILMS FROG, 3. BOWLER FEEDS FERRET, 4. BULLDOG FREES FAIRY, 5. BICYCLIST FINDS FORTUNE, 6. BEES FRIGHTEN FAMILY, 7. BAKER FANS FEET.

Prepared by the Book Division

Nancy Laties Feresten, *Vice President, Editor in Chief, Children's Books*

Jonathan Halling, *Design Director, Children's Publishing*

Jennifer Emmett, *Executive Editor, Reference and Solo, Children's Books*

Carl Mehler, *Director of Maps*

R. Gary Colbert, *Production Director*

Jennifer A. Thornton, *Managing Editor*

Staff for This Book

Robin Terry, *Project Editor*

Eva Absher, *Art Direction and Design*

Lori Epstein, *Illustrations Editor*

Grace Hill, *Associate Managing Editor*

Jeff Reynolds, *Marketing Director, Children's Books*

Lewis R. Bassford, *Production Manager*

Susan Borke, *Legal and Business Affairs*

Based on the "Fun Stuff" department in NATIONAL GEOGRAPHIC KIDS magazine

Jonathan Halling, *Design Director*

Robin Terry, *Senior Editor*

Nicole M. Lazarus, *Associate Art Director*

Kelley Miller, *Photo Editor*

Erin Monroney, *Writer-Researcher*

Manufacturing and Quality Management

Christopher A. Liedel, *Chief Financial Officer*

Phillip L. Schlosser, *Vice President*

Chris Brown, *Technical Director*

Rachel Faulise, *Manufacturing Manager*

Nicole Elliott, *Manufacturing Manager*